ADVENT

Kerstin Niehoff   Laura Fleiter

ADVENT

Recipes and crafts for the
countdown to Christmas

murdoch books

Sydney | London

"SAVING THE BEST FOR LAST – HELLO, DECEMBER!"

Being true fans of winter, we're only too happy to settle into the season of snuggling up at home. For us, our levels of anticipation start rising in autumn, as we farewell the warmer months. We love it when the air gets cooler and the wind blows leaves through the parks; when we enjoy the comfort of our homes in the early dusk and make the best of this peaceful time by cooking, by exploring our creative sides, or by just resting – things that we often don't make time for in the excitement of summer.

Not everybody finds it easy to make friends with winter, but it's definitely worthwhile to embrace it, to engage with it, to give it meaning and to reset our priorities. Let's dedicate winter to everything we really care about: let's pay attention to each other, let's take time out for ourselves and our thoughts, and let's share our valuable time with family and friends.

This book wants to inspire you to fill the often busy pre-Christmas period with a sense of serenity and joy. We deliberately haven't included any of the conventional Christmas kitsch because we wanted to focus on this magical time in all of its authentic glory. We invite you to recast the lead-up to Christmas as a time for finding and creating delightfully quiet moments and a sense of belonging. May the thoughts, recipes, DIY ideas and carefully selected photos in this book remind you of all the little things that make this season so special.

We're very happy that this book has found its way into your hands. Make yourself comfortable and enjoy it in the moment, wherever you may be.

We wish you a magnificent pre-Christmas season.

5

CONTENTS

FOR ME

WINTER HAS COME
AND EMBRACES US FONDLY...

Winter may look dreary at first sight, but when you look closer, it's actually nature taking a rest in a deep and peaceful sleep. It's as if nature is taking time out to recover from months and months of busy, long days. Time to stop and take a deep, nurturing breath.

What if we did the same? If we slowed down for once in the flow of seasons and allowed ourselves to take a deep breath of fresh, cool air or enjoy the moment in the glow of a few candles? If we just rested in ourselves and the present?

Winter is the time when we love to stay warm indoors with a comfy blanket around our shoulders and a mug of hot chocolate between our palms. When we listen to the soft sound of raindrops tapping on our windows and watch them sliding down the glass. Winter is the time when, if we're lucky, snow covers our world in a blanket of glittering white and muffles the noise of our lives. Each one of these quiet days is an invitation to slow down.

As we near the end of the year, we might find ourselves drawn to reflection. While we continue to live our normal, everyday lives and the pre-Christmas season can become very hectic, we can still dot our days with moments of serenity by paying attention to the little joys of life such as the glitter of morning frost on trees and lawns or the incomparable pleasure of sitting by a roaring open fire. Let's enjoy the touch of peaceful melancholy on clear days when our breath rises in puffs of white. Let's remember how exciting the magical weeks leading up to Christmas felt when we were children. This is the time for time – for ourselves and each other. The time to make peace and let go of past events. The time for making new memories.

FOR
ME

ome – quickly. Out of the cold and into the warmth. Shoes off, coat on the hook, track pants on. The world will have to stay outside. A match gently lighting a few candles and then – peace. A deep breath in the flickering light. 'Me' time.

It's the perfect time to relax, to cast off all the pressure and stimulation that we're bombarded with each day. As we've become permanently available, it's become less and less common for us to consciously spend time by ourselves. We often rush through each day, are much too harsh on ourselves and keep going, just to meet our own expectations as well as those of others. All this rushing can leave us with little time for checking in with ourselves. Time flies, and there are only rare glimpses of clarity, which are all too often drowned out by the next distraction before we've even really noticed them. It's up to us whether we allow ourselves to be consumed by the demands of the outside world or consciously decide to resist. Christmas is the holiday of love, and that includes love for ourselves, which so often falls by the wayside.

Often it's in the winter months, when the sun is weak and the weather doesn't encourage a lot of outdoor activity, that we notice how tired we have become in body and spirit. These months are the time for resting and recuperating. Winter is when we can treat ourselves to slowing down, to a second helping of our favourite home-cooked food and a more relaxed approach to doing what needs to be done. A quiet moment of reflection on the events of the year helps us to let go and arrive fully in the here and now. Let's make ourselves comfortable, let's cook and make space for creativity. Let's be kind to ourselves and enjoy this kindness with all of our senses. When else, if not in the weeks before Christmas?

WINTER BREAKFAST BOWL WITH SPICED COOKIE CRUMBS

How about a winter edition of the ever-popular breakfast bowl, made of
unforgettably creamy oats with cinnamon and spiced cookie crumbs?
Just the thing to get you into the mood of the season.

Serves 1

2 bananas
1 apple
½ tsp ground cinnamon
2 tbsp milk
1 tbsp quick-cooking oats
2 tsp almond butter
3 pitted dates
2 spiced spekulatius cookies
1 tsp dried cranberries

Peel and slice one banana. Transfer to the freezer to chill for
at least 8 hours.

Halve the apple and remove the core. Peel the second banana.
Blend the frozen banana slices with the fresh banana, one apple
half, cinnamon, milk, oats, almond butter and dates. Transfer
the mixture to a serving bowl.

Thinly slice the other apple half. Place the cookies in a freezer
bag and bash them into crumbs with a rolling pin. Garnish the
blended banana and oat mixture with the apple slices, cookie
crumbs and cranberries.

TIP

Feel free to vary the toppings to your liking.
Nuts and different types of fruit make perfect choices.

FRENCH PANCAKES WITH PLUM COMPOTE

A delectable combination of the all-time breakfast favourites
French toast and pancakes: festive brioche pikelets topped with
warm plum compote. For a special Advent morning just for you.

Serves 1
For the plum compote:
100 g (3½ oz) tinned pitted
 plums
1 pinch ground vanilla

For the French pancakes:
200 ml (7 fl oz) milk
1 egg
1 tbsp pure maple syrup
1 pinch ground cinnamon
2 small brioche buns
2 tbsp vegetable oil

For the plum compote, coarsely blend the plums with some
of the liquid from the tin. Transfer to a small saucepan, place
over low heat and gently simmer to reduce the mixture a little.
Stir in the vanilla. Keep warm until serving.

For the French pancakes, whisk the milk with the egg, maple
syrup and cinnamon. Halve the brioche buns and press between
your palms to flatten them. Dip the brioche halves into the milk
and egg mixture for about 1 minute each, turning once. Heat the
oil in a frying pan over low heat. Add the brioche halves and fry
until golden, flipping over to cook evenly on both sides.

Stack the warm French pancakes on a plate and top with the
plum compote.

TIP

These pancakes are also wonderful with blueberries or sliced apples.
Feel free to vary the fruit to your liking.

MAPLE-ROASTED VEGGIES WITH POLENTA

Rustic and just amazing – a colourful mix of veggies,
oven-roasted to perfection and served with creamy polenta.
Healthy eating can be so simple, and so delicious.

Serves 1
For the roasted veggies:
1 beetroot
1 carrot
1 red onion
6 sprigs fresh thyme
1 tbsp olive oil
Sea salt flakes
Freshly ground black pepper
1 tbsp pure maple syrup

For the polenta:
100 ml (3½ fl oz) vegetable
  stock
100 ml (3½ fl oz) milk
40 g (1½ oz) polenta
10 g (¼ oz) parmesan cheese
1 tbsp olive oil
Sea salt
Freshly ground black pepper

For the roasted veggies, preheat the oven to 250°C (500°F). Peel and slice the beetroot and carrot. Peel the onion and cut into wedges. Pick and finely chop the leaves off four sprigs of thyme. Toss the vegetables with the chopped thyme, olive oil, sea salt, pepper and maple syrup and spread out on a baking tray. Bake until lightly caramelised, about 15 minutes.

While the vegetables are roasting, cook the polenta. Combine the vegetable stock and milk in a saucepan and bring to the boil. Whisk in the polenta, then gently simmer for 15–20 minutes. Grate the parmesan and stir into the polenta with the olive oil. Season with salt and pepper.

Transfer the polenta to a bowl and arrange the veggies on top. Garnish with the remaining thyme sprigs.

TIP

You can also cook the veggies in a frying pan, but their flavour develops much better in the oven, and you'll also need less oil.

PORRIDGE WITH ORANGE SEGMENTS

A steaming hot bowl of porridge in the morning is a perfect, soothing start for any day – even more so when our palate wakes up to the taste of sweet dates, juicy oranges and vanilla. This is comfort food at its indulgent best.

Serves 1

3 pitted medjool dates
1 tbsp almond butter
1 pinch ground vanilla
1 pinch sea salt
150 ml (5 fl oz) milk
4 tbsp quick-cooking oats
½ orange
½ tsp cocoa nibs

Blend the dates, almond butter, vanilla, salt and milk with 2 tablespoons water to make a smooth mixture. Transfer to a small saucepan and bring to the boil over high heat. Whisk in the oats. Reduce the heat to medium and continue to simmer for about 1 minute. Remove from the heat.

Carefully peel the orange half with a sharp knife, removing all of the white pith. Separate the orange segments by slicing along the thin membranes.

Transfer the porridge to a bowl, top with the orange segments, garnish with the cocoa nibs and enjoy warm.

TIP

This soothing porridge also goes wonderfully with stewed apricots or mandarin segments.

ROASTED PEAR WITH HONEY & ROSEMARY

Juicy pear, drizzled with honey and served on crusty sourdough bread
with delicately seasoned feta and a sprinkle of aromatic rosemary.
It's the perfect dish for everyone permanently torn between sweet and
savoury – a delicious snack and a fantastic entrée.

Serves 1

1 pear
2 tsp honey
1 sprig fresh rosemary
2 small slices of
* sourdough bread*
2 tsp butter
1 pinch sea salt
25 g (1 oz) feta cheese

Preheat the oven to 200°C (400°F). Slice the pear lengthways.
Place the pear slices on a baking tray lined with baking paper.
Drizzle with the honey and bake for about 10 minutes.

Meanwhile, pick and finely chop the rosemary leaves.

Spread the sourdough slices with the butter. Heat a frying
pan over medium heat and toast the sourdough on both sides.
Remove from the pan and sprinkle with sea salt. Crumble the
feta over the toasted sourdough and top with the roasted pear
slices. Transfer to a plate, sprinkle with the chopped rosemary
and enjoy.

TIP

The roasted pear is also delicious entirely by itself or in a salad of leafy greens.

ADVENT

IN WINTER WOODS A HERD OF SNOWFLAKES
IS GUIDED BY THE SHEPHERD BREEZE
AND ONE FIR TREE ANTICIPATES
THE BLESSING IT WILL SOON RECEIVE
AND LISTENS FOR IT, STRETCHES EVERY LIMB
TOWARD THE SNOW-BRIGHT PATHS — PRIMED
AND GROWING OUT, AGAINST THE WIND,
TO GREET THE VERY NIGHT OF THE DIVINE.

— RAINER MARIA RILKE,
TRANS. CHRISTOPHER NEWTON

WINTER SALAD WITH HONEYED NUTS

Quick to prepare and incredibly healthy! Crisp, fresh green leaves meet crunchy nuts and a fruity dressing – a winter dream for salad lovers and a welcome balance to all those heavy winter foods.

Serves 1

For the honeyed nuts:
25 g (1 oz) cashews
25 g (1 oz) walnuts
25 g (1 oz) hazelnuts
1 tbsp honey
Sea salt

For the salad:
40 g (1½ oz) lamb's lettuce
30 g (1 oz) radicchio
½ apple
1 mandarin

For the dressing:
1 tbsp cranberry juice
1 tsp honey
1 tbsp olive oil
1 tsp mustard
Sea salt
Freshly ground black pepper

Lightly toast the nuts in a hot, dry frying pan. Add the honey and stir to ensure that the walnuts are evenly coated (be careful not to burn the honey). Season with a little sea salt. Remove the pan from the heat after about 1 minute. Transfer the nuts to a plate and refrigerate them briefly.

For the salad, trim and wash the lamb's lettuce and radicchio. Thinly slice the radicchio. Remove the core from the apple half and slice. Peel the mandarin and divide it into segments. Add the lamb's lettuce, radicchio, apple and mandarin to a bowl.

For the dressing, whisk the cranberry juice, honey, olive oil and mustard together and season with salt and pepper.

Carefully combine the salad with the dressing and serve topped with the honeyed nuts.

TIP

The honeyed nuts make a fabulous snack for a relaxed winter's night on the couch.

BAKED FLATBREAD WITH KALE & SALAMI OR SMOKED TOFU

What could be better than a deliciously crusty, baked flatbread
served straight out of the oven? This tastes best eaten
with your fingers right off a wooden board.

Makes 1 flatbread
For the dough:
⅓ cup (50 g) plain
   (all-purpose) flour
1 tbsp olive oil
25 ml (¾ fl oz) warm water
1 egg yolk
½ tsp sea salt

For the topping:
50 g (1¾ oz) block of salami
   or smoked tofu
1 tbsp vegetable oil as
   required
1 handful baby kale leaves
1 small red onion
100 g (3½ oz) crème fraîche
Sea salt
Freshly ground black pepper

Preheat the oven to 200°C (400°F). For the dough, combine
the flour and oil with the warm water, egg yolk and salt, either
by hand or using an electric mixer fitted with a dough hook.
Process until the mixture is pliable and no longer sticky. Add
a little more flour if necessary. Transfer the dough to a sheet of
baking paper and roll it out until about 3 mm (⅛ inch) thick.
Slide the baking paper and dough onto a baking tray.

Dice the salami or smoked tofu. Briefly fry the tofu in vegetable
oil in a frying pan. Wash and trim the kale and cut it into strips.
Halve and thinly slice the onion. Season the crème fraîche with
salt and pepper, then spread it on the prepared dough. Top the
flatbread with the kale strips, onion and diced salami or tofu.

Bake the flatbread until it is browned around the edges, about
15–20 minutes. Transfer to a board, cut into slices and serve hot.

TIP

Feel free to vary the flatbread toppings with your favourite
winter ingredients. Finely diced dried fruit, for example,
tastes amazing and creates a distinctly festive flavour.

ALMOND MILK & CINNAMON COFFEE

The seductive aroma of fresh coffee, almonds and cinnamon from a mug of this delicious concoction will warm your hands and soul. A glorious start to an Advent morning.

Serves 1

50 g (1¾ oz) almonds
½ tsp ground cinnamon,
  plus a little extra for
  garnish
1 pinch sea salt
2 pitted dates
Ground coffee for 1 espresso

Cover the almonds with water and leave to soak for 1–2 hours. Drain and transfer the soaked almonds to a blender together with 300 ml (10½ fl oz) fresh water. Blend thoroughly. Add the cinnamon, salt and dates and blend again. Line a strainer with a nut milk bag, a piece of muslin or a thin tea towel. Strain the almond mixture, squeezing to extract the liquid and collect the pulp-free milk.

Prepare your favourite espresso. (We like to use a traditional Italian espresso maker, but you can use your preferred method.)

Warm the almond milk, lightly froth with a milk frother and pour the milk into a mug. Add the espresso and sprinkle with a little extra cinnamon.

TIP

You can substitute ready-made almond milk, of course, but you'll definitely taste the difference – home-made almond milk is quite addictive.

BE KIND TO YOURSELF!
TAKE TIME OUT,
   HUM A FEW CHRISTMAS CAROLS
   AND ENJOY THE MOMENT
         WITH ALL OF YOUR SENSES.
PRECIOUS MOMENTS
   FULL OF PEACE AND WONDER.

RED CABBAGE & POTATO SOUP

Bring some colour to your plate! This recipe shows off red cabbage,
a classic winter vegetable, in a very different light, as a wonderfully
warming soup with a comforting aroma for cold days.

Serves 1

1 onion
½ garlic clove
1 potato
100 g (3½ oz) red cabbage
2 tbsp olive oil
½ tbsp balsamic vinegar,
    plus a little extra for
    seasoning
300 ml (10½ fl oz) vegetable
    stock
1 tsp pistachios
Sea salt
Freshly ground black pepper
2 tsp honey
1 tsp almond butter

Dice the onion and crush the garlic. Peel and dice the potato. Trim and dice the cabbage. Heat the oil in a saucepan over low heat. Add the onion and garlic and briefly sweat. Add the potato and cabbage and sauté until softened. Deglaze the pan with the balsamic vinegar. Pour in the stock and simmer the soup for 15 minutes.

Chop the pistachios. Purée the soup with a stick blender or upright blender. Season with salt, pepper, honey and more balsamic vinegar to taste and transfer to a serving bowl. Garnish with the almond butter and pistachios.

TIP

Substitute the honey with agave syrup, pure
maple syrup or sugar to make this a vegan delight.

HOT WINTER SMOOTHIE

Beat the winter blues with this warming smoothie full of
healthy ingredients. It will warm your soul and brighten your mood,
sip by sip, as you relax in your favourite armchair.

Serves 1
100 ml (3½ fl oz) oat milk
1 banana
2 tsp hazelnut butter
1 tbsp unsweetened cocoa
*   powder*
1 tsp linseeds
1 pinch sea salt
50 ml (1½ fl oz) coconut milk
½ tsp locust bean gum
1 pinch ground vanilla
1 pinch raw sugar
Chocolate shavings,
*   for garnish*

Heat the oat milk in a small saucepan. Place the banana,
hazelnut butter, cocoa powder, linseeds and salt in a blender.
Add the hot oat milk and blend until smooth. Return the
mixture to the saucepan and keep warm over low heat.

Add the coconut milk, locust bean gum, vanilla and sugar
to a tall beaker. Whisk with a stick blender until the mixture
turns foamy and firms up, similar to whipped cream – this
may take several minutes.

Pour the hot smoothie into a mug, top with the whipped
coconut cream and serve garnished with chocolate shavings.

TIP

If you double the amount of locust bean gum and blend
everything together, you'll get an amazing chocolate custard.

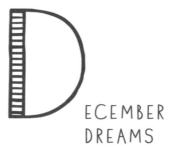

ECEMBER
DREAMS

ADVENT CANDLES

Minimalist beauty in no time: creating an Advent mood doesn't take much effort. And who's to say that you must have an Advent wreath? Beautiful bottles make perfect candle holders. Fill them with your favourite objects to create something that's uniquely you.

Label printer or permanent marker/glass marker
4 bottles
4 sprigs of greenery, such as eucalyptus, holly or spruce
4 candles

Use a label printer to make four labels: 'one', 'two', 'three' and 'four'. Stick them on the bottles. Alternatively, use a glass marker or permanent marker to label the bottles. White looks particularly elegant and sophisticated.

Fill the bottles with water and place a sprig of greenery into each bottle, making sure that they are completely covered with water.

Push the candles into the bottle openings. If necessary, use a small knife to trim the candle ends a little so that they just fit inside the bottles.

DOOR WREATH

Making a Christmas wreath is an almost meditative exercise.
Put on some music, pour yourself a cup of tea and breathe in the
scent of your favourite greenery. All you need is a little space, time
and a small selection of materials. Switch off your mental chatter
and turn on your creativity. You'll be proud of the result.

1 bunch eucalyptus stems
2 bunches fir (e.g. silver,
    Nordmann, blue noble
    or Nikko fir), spruce
    (common or blue spruce),
    thuja or false cypress
    stems, or similar greenery
Green florists' wire
1 straw wreath
Natural decorations,
    such as pine cones or
    beauty-heads
Glue gun (optional)

Trim all stems to about the same length and lay them
out within easy reach, sorted by type. Insert one end
of the wire into the straw frame and wind the wire
around the frame once to make sure it holds firmly.
Attach the foliage to the frame, one stem at a time, in
an overlapping pattern so that the stems are covered.
Secure each stem with wire. It's best not to trim the
wire after adding each stem, but to continue winding
it around the wreath.

Use dense foliage such as fir at the bottom to make sure
that the frame is entirely covered, and work with more
delicate greenery at the top. Be careful to hide the wire
between your greenery as you wrap it. Once you have
completed your wreath, trim off the wire generously
and push the end deep into the straw frame so that it
won't come loose.

For the final touch, add a few decorative elements,
attaching them either with wire or a glue gun. If your
wreath still looks a little thin, insert a few more stems
or loosen up a few spots.

TIP

Look for beautiful decorations straight out of nature
during your next walk or hike in the forest. Keep your
eyes open – who knows what treasures you'll find?

CHRISTMAS SCENT

A delicate, festive scent can create a cosy atmosphere in any room and quietly accompany us throughout the Advent season – without any chemicals. Make this scent as a treat for yourself or as a lovely little gift for the holiday season.

½ orange
1 preserving jar, about
  600 ml (21 fl oz)
2 cinnamon sticks
About 10 cloves
3 star anise

Thinly slice the orange and add the slices to the jar. Add the remaining ingredients, fill the jar with boiling water and immediately seal it. Set aside for about 3 days to allow the aroma to develop.

Open the jar and place it in a warm spot or on top of a teapot warmer to allow the aroma to spread.

TIP

Prepare a few jars at a time so you'll have enough of this beautifully festive scent for several rooms.

C LARITY

FOR
YOU

When was the last time you had a deep and honest talk with somebody, face to face, that went beyond small talk? Whether with our friends, families or in other relationships, it's far too rarely that we take the time to really listen to, hear and see others. We're always on the go, our thoughts three steps ahead of us, engaged with what's next in our lives, and as a result we miss out on each other. December is the perfect month to pay attention to everything we didn't make enough time for throughout the year.

There's nothing more valuable that we could give to each other than time – in whichever form, whether a long overdue phone call with words spoken from the heart; a small gift, home-made with a lot of attention to detail; or a lovely dinner sharing friendship, time and food until late in the night. Bringing joy to the people we love is good for our souls and creates moments that we'll remember forever with a deep sense of gratitude.

During Advent, we can make space for these precious encounters by consciously refusing to be absorbed by consumerism, by spending time together, listening to each other and expressing our gratitude. None of this should be taken for granted.

Do good to each other…

ORANGE & CINNAMON SYRUP

Each drop of this sweet and fruity concoction is a divine little dream that makes everything a bit more delicious. It's perfect for flavouring your favourite hot beverage, or as a sauce for desserts, or as a spread for toast and much more. Stirred into hot milk, it makes an amazing night cap for cold winter evenings.

Makes 1 small bottle (about 200 ml/7 fl oz)

1 orange, or 100 ml (3½ fl oz) orange juice
200 g (7 oz) raw sugar
3 tsp ground cinnamon

Squeeze the orange and transfer the juice to a measuring cup. Add enough water to make 200 ml (7 fl oz). Strain the liquid into a small saucepan. Whisk in the raw sugar and cinnamon. Bring to the boil, then reduce the heat to low and simmer for 8–10 minutes.

Transfer the syrup into a small, clean bottle and set aside to cool before sealing.

Stored in a cool, dark place, this syrup will keep for at least 2 months.

TIP

If you make this as a gift, add a little handwritten card explaining some different ways to use the syrup, for example in coffee, as a delicious pancake topping or in a festive cocktail. Tie the card to the bottle with some ribbon or twine.

WHITE CINNAMON & ALMOND CRACKLES

A perfect combination of fragrant cinnamon and white chocolate. If you want to use these crackles as a gift, we suggest you make enough for yourself as well. Otherwise they might never make it to the intended recipient...

Makes about 20

¾ cup (100 g) slivered almonds

200 g (7 oz) white cooking chocolate

4 tbsp puffed quinoa

½ tsp ground cinnamon

1 pinch sea salt

Toast the slivered almonds in a dry frying pan over medium heat. Melt the white chocolate in a heatproof bowl sitting over a saucepan of simmering water.

Combine the quinoa puffs and almonds with the cinnamon and salt. Stir the mixture into the melted chocolate.

Line a baking tray with baking paper. Use a teaspoon to scoop spoonfuls of the chocolate and almond mixture onto the tray. Leave to set completely.

Transfer the crackles to pretty boxes or a cookie tin. They will keep for 1–2 months if they're tightly sealed.

TIP

Allow your creativity to go wild with this recipe.
Use different types of nuts or seeds with the remaining
ingredients to make your very own crackles recipe.

PEANUT BRITTLE

A crunchy, nutty delight for all those who love nut brittle and sweets. This recipe is a perfect alternative to Christmas cookies with an afternoon tea or coffee.

Makes about 12

1⅔ cups (250 g) unsalted
   peanuts
4 tbsp maple syrup
200 g (7 oz) sugar
1 tbsp butter
1 pinch baking powder
Sea salt flakes

Coarsely chop the peanuts and dry-roast in a frying pan over high heat until they start to take on colour. Remove the peanuts from the pan.

Reduce the heat to medium and add the maple syrup, sugar, butter and 4 tablespoons of water to the pan. Whisk until the mixture turns creamy, but stop stirring as soon as it starts to boil. Simmer for 5–8 minutes until the mixture turns darker. Add the peanuts and briefly toss them in the pan so that they are covered with the maple syrup mixture. Stir in the baking powder with a wooden spoon. Keep stirring until the mixture starts to firm up.

Carefully transfer the mixture to a tray lined with baking paper and level the surface with the wooden spoon. Sprinkle with sea salt flakes and leave to cool completely.

Once the peanut brittle has cooled and hardened, break it into pieces and transfer it to a jar or cookie tin.

Stored in a tin or jar in a dry, dark place, the peanut brittle will keep for 1–2 months.

TIP

You can substitute any type of nuts you have in your pantry for this recipe, or choose your favourite nuts.

PUMPKIN & APRICOT CHUTNEY

This chutney is addictive! If you love to treat your family and friends to very special home-made gifts, this recipe is for you. Enjoyed with an aromatic cheese and crisp crackers, this chutney will have the lucky recipients floating on culinary cloud nine.

Makes 1 small jar (about 200 ml/7 fl oz)

125 g (4½ oz) peeled pumpkin (squash)
¼ onion
25 g (1 oz) dried apricots
About 2 cm (¾ inch) piece fresh ginger
25 g (1 oz) sultanas
40 g (1½ oz) brown sugar
75 ml (2¼ fl oz) white wine vinegar

Dice the pumpkin. Finely dice the onion. Finely dice the apricots. Peel and finely grate the ginger.

Combine all the ingredients in a saucepan. Simmer over low heat for 1–1½ hours until the pumpkin has softened and almost all of the liquid has evaporated.

Transfer the hot chutney straight to a clean jar and seal the jar tightly. The chutney will keep for at least 3 months.

TIP

Decorate the jar with a hand-made label suggesting possible uses for the chutney to make it an even more delightful gift.

SNOW BITES

Healthy snacking during Advent? Of course it's possible! Every bite of these soft little snowy balls enchants the senses, without any added sugar. They're an ideal gift for those among your family and friends who like to limit the sweet treats around Christmas.

Makes about 12

½ cup (50 g) quick-cooking oats
⅔ cup (100 g) cashews
3 tbsp agave syrup
1 pinch ground vanilla
1 pinch sea salt
4 tbsp desiccated coconut

Add the oats and cashews to a food processor or blender and blend until you have a fine meal. Add the agave syrup, vanilla, salt and 1 tablespoon water and blend again briefly.

Transfer the mixture to a bowl. Combine with 2 tablespoons of the desiccated coconut and shape into small balls. Roll the balls in the remaining coconut.

Stored in a tin or jar in the refrigerator, the snow bites will keep for about a week.

TIP

Feel free to substitute the cashews for a different type of nut.

LOVE THY NEIGHBOUR

JOY IS PRECIOUS AND GROWS
AS WE SHARE IT.
LET'S HELP SPREAD JOY,
LET'S WARM HEARTS AND
CREATE HARMONY
BY GIFTING SMALL GESTURES
AND OFFERING HELPING HANDS.

DOUBLE-CHOCOLATE COOKIES

What food is absolutely essential for the Christmas spirit?
Chocolate, of course! These pretty little cookies will delight
every chocolate lover.

Makes about 20

100 g (3½ oz) cold butter
100 g (3½ oz) raw sugar
½ tsp ground vanilla
1 cup (150 g) spelt flour, plus
*   extra for dusting*
½ tsp baking powder
4 tbsp unsweetened cocoa
*   powder*
½ cup (50 g) almond meal
2 eggs
50 g (1¾ oz) white cooking
*   chocolate*

Preheat the oven to 175°C (345°F). Dice the butter and place in
the bowl of an electric mixer fitted with a dough hook. Add the
sugar, vanilla, flour, baking powder, cocoa, almond meal and
eggs. Quickly combine to make a smooth dough.

Roll out the dough about 5 mm (¼ inch) thick on a lightly
floured surface. Cut out your favourite shapes and transfer to a
baking tray lined with baking paper. Bake the cookies for about
12 minutes. Transfer to a wire rack and leave to cool completely.

Chop the chocolate. Gently melt the chocolate in a heatproof
bowl set over a pan of simmering water. Transfer to a piping bag
with a narrow nozzle. Decorate the cookies with the chocolate.

These chocolate cookies will keep for about 3 months in a tin.
Make sure that the tin seals well to keep the cookies dry. Most
likely they'll be gone well before Christmas, though!

TIP

If you don't have a piping bag, make your own by snipping off one corner
of a freezer bag to create a hole with a diameter of about 3 mm (⅛ inch).

GRINCH COOKIES

What could you possibly serve a Christmas fiend such as the Grinch? We've got a suggestion: delicious, chewy cookies dyed Grinch green with matcha. An exciting version of classic chocolate chip cookies with a delectably soft centre.

Makes about 15

½ cup (125 g) butter, softened

130 g (4½ oz) raw sugar

1 egg

½ tsp ground vanilla

140 g (5 oz) plain (all-purpose) flour

2 tsp matcha powder

½ tsp bicarbonate of soda (baking soda)

½ tsp sea salt

150 g (5½ oz) milk chocolate

Preheat the oven to 190°C (375°F). Place the butter and sugar in a mixing bowl and beat until creamy, about 3 minutes, with a hand whisk or a hand mixer. Add the egg and vanilla and continue to beat for another 3 minutes.

Sift the flour, matcha powder, bicarbonate of soda and salt into the mixture and gently fold in with a spatula. Coarsely chop the chocolate and fold it into the cookie dough.

Place small heaps of the dough (about 2 tablespoons each) onto a baking tray lined with baking paper. Leave them as mounds; don't flatten them. Bake for 7–10 minutes until the edges start to brown. Remove from the oven and leave to cool on the tray for a few minutes, as the cookies will still be very soft just after baking. Transfer to a wire rack and leave to cool completely.

Stored in a cookie tin or a jar in a cool, dry place, the cookies will keep for 2–3 months.

TIP

Top these cookies with white chocolate and macadamia nuts for an amazing alternative.

TOASTED PEPITAS

As unlikely as it sounds, there are people who aren't fond of sweet treats. But we have a solution for them. These home-made savoury nibbles are ideal for movie nights spent under a cosy blanket on a comfortable sofa.

Makes 1 small gift bag

250 g (9 oz) pepitas
   (pumpkin seeds)
2 tsp raw sugar
2 tsp sea salt
½ tsp garlic powder
¼ tsp sweet paprika
1 pinch freshly ground
   black pepper
2 tsp coconut oil

Preheat the oven to 150°C (300°F). Spread the pepitas on a baking tray lined with baking paper. Toast in the oven for about 5 minutes until they start to pop.

Mix the sugar, salt, garlic powder, paprika, pepper and coconut oil into a paste. Mix with the roasted pepitas, stirring until well coated. Roast the pepitas for another 5–10 minutes. Transfer to a bowl and cool completely.

Kept in a sealed jar, such as a nice preserving jar, the toasted seeds will keep for 1–2 months.

TIP

Feel free to be creative with these toasted pepitas and use any seasoning mix you like. Curry powder goes very well with pepitas, for example.

ATTENTION
AND APPRECIATION –
IT'S OFTEN THE LITTLE
THINGS THAT HAVE
A LOT OF MEANING
AND HELP US TO
TRULY CONNECT.

GINGERBREAD CHRISTMAS TREE

Gingerbread, that most traditional of baked Christmas goodies, invites us to get really creative. Sometimes it might even turn out almost too pretty to eat – but you should, as this recipe really tastes fabulous.

Makes 1

For the dough:
125 g (4½ oz) honey
50 g (1¾ oz) raw sugar
65 g (2¼ oz) butter
1⅔ cups (250 g) plain (all-purpose) flour, plus extra for dusting
½ tsp baking powder
15 g (½ oz) packet gingerbread spice (or home-made spice mix, see tip below)
1 tbsp unsweetened cocoa powder
1 egg

For the glaze:
100 g (3½ oz) icing (confectioners') sugar

To make the dough, add the honey, sugar and butter to a small saucepan and bring to the boil. Remove from the heat.

Combine the flour, baking powder, gingerbread spice and cocoa in a mixing bowl. Using an electric mixer fitted with a dough hook, combine the flour mixture, honey mixture, egg and 2 tablespoons water to make a smooth dough. Add a little more water if the dough seems too dry. Wrap the dough in plastic wrap and refrigerate for 2 hours.

Preheat the oven to 180°C (350°F). Roll out the dough on a lightly floured surface until 5 mm (¼ inch) thick. Use a sharp knife to cut out a Christmas tree shape. Shape or cut the rest of the dough as you like. Put the tree and remaining cookie shapes on a baking tray lined with baking paper. Bake for 15 minutes. Remove from the oven, transfer to a wire rack and leave to cool completely.

For the glaze, whisk the icing sugar and 2–3 tablespoons water until smooth. Add a little more water if you can still see lumps of sugar. Glaze the cooled gingerbread tree and remaining cookies to your taste.

TIP

For home-made gingerbread spice, combine 35 g (1¼ oz) ground cinnamon, 9 g (¼ oz) ground cloves and 2 g (¹⁄₁₆ oz) each of ground coriander, ground allspice, ground ginger, ground cardamom and ground nutmeg. Stored in a dry place away from light, the mixture will keep for at least 1 year.

CARAMELISED
TURMERIC WALNUTS

Glittering lights and fresh, hot Vienna almonds are among the things embodying the unique charm of a stroll through a Christmas market. If that's not on offer for you (or if it's not something you fancy), make yourself comfortable at home and enjoy home-made sweet nuts. Feel free to experiment with different types of nuts – they all taste delicious freshly toasted and delicately seasoned with turmeric.

Makes 1 small gift bag
200 g (7 oz) sugar
½ tsp ground vanilla
1 pinch sea salt
1 pinch ground turmeric
1⅔ cups (200 g) walnuts

Add the sugar, vanilla, sea salt and turmeric to a frying pan. Pour in 100 ml (3½ fl oz) water and stir to combine. Bring to a simmer without stirring. Add the walnuts. Increase the heat and continue to boil, stirring continuously, until the liquid has evaporated. Reduce the heat again and continue to stir until the sugar firms up again.

Spread the caramelised nuts on a baking tray lined with baking paper and leave to cool.

Stored in a well-sealed container in a dry place, the caramelised walnuts will keep for 1–2 months.

TIP

Substitute cinnamon for the turmeric if you're after a more traditional flavour.

S

ERENITY IS A WORD
TO KEEP IN MIND THROUGHOUT ADVENT.
THIS IS THE TIME FOR QUIET REFLECTION,
FOR CHANGING OUR PERSPECTIVE ON THINGS,
FOR RECOGNISING THE BOUNDLESS JOY
THAT RESTS IN THE LITTLE THINGS.

GIFT
WRAPPING

It's the same story year after year – your precious gifts need to
be wrapped! For some, this is a fun and creative task, while others
couldn't be happier to have their gifts wrapped in the store.
Unfortunately, a lot of commercial wrapping paper is anything
but sustainable. And sustainability is worth a thought or two,
considering that most presents are torn open and the wrapping
paper is thrown straight into the recycling bin. One option is to
wrap your gifts in pretty fabrics or scarves, which adds a generous
touch. Or read on for an alternative to conventional wrapping paper.

*Black hand-made sustainable
or natural paper (available
online or from art supply
shops)*
Adhesive tape or glue
Cypress stems
Paintbrush
White craft paint
*Light-coloured natural string
or twine*

Carefully wrap your gift in the natural paper.

Arrange evenly sized cypress stems in a star pattern on
top of the wrapped gift and attach them with a piece of
tape or a little glue. Once all stems are in place, decorate
the top with dots and splashes of paint by dipping the
paintbrush into the paint, holding a finger horizontally
above the gift and firmly tapping the top of the finger
with the brush a few times just below the bristles for
better control. You might want to try this out on plain
paper first to get a feel for it. Leave the paint to dry.

Wrap the natural string or twine around the gift a few
times, just below the cypress stems. Tie the string at the
back of the gift. Finish by sliding a photo, gift card or
postcard underneath the string.

WATERCOLOUR CHRISTMAS CARDS

Personalised cards for any occasion? Not a problem if you make them yourself. It's not only fun, but also makes for very special cards. Give it a go, even if you don't think you have any talent.

Fine pencil
Eraser
A5 watercolour paper
Glass of water
Small paintbrushes
Watercolours in white and shades of green
Mixing palette
Fine dark green or black felt tip pen

Sketch out a Christmas tree on the watercolour paper using a fine pencil. Use a favourite photo as inspiration.

Next, carefully dampen the surface you want to paint on with a little water. Then dip your paintbrush into water and your watercolours to mix the shade of green you want on your palette. Start painting in thin strokes along the outer contours of the tree and let the colour bleed towards the inside. Then gently brush the water across the areas to be filled to spread the colour. Be careful not to use too much water; otherwise it gets difficult to control the spread of the colour.

Use gentle, dabbing strokes of the brush and a little of a different shade of green to add in the branches. Leave the watercolour to dry.

If you like, apply a few highlights to put the finishing touches on your watercolours. Dot the upper edges of the branches with white paint. Add greetings of your choice using a fine pen and your best handwriting.

4-TREAT ADVENT CALENDAR

Making an Advent calendar for a loved one has a long tradition.
We think it doesn't always have to include a treat for every day.
If you only include four little gifts, it's much easier to make them
really special. One little bag for each Advent Sunday, filled with
a little surprise each, to be grandly revealed in company.

1 twig (e.g. birch)
*Twine (e.g. black, or black
 and white)*
2 nails
Hammer
Plain-coloured jute
Scissors
Black cardboard
Hole punch
White permanent marker
*Foliage, stars, etc.,
 for decorating*

Attach a piece of twine, each about 10 cm (4 inches)
long, to the ends of the twig. Tie the twine ends to make
loops. Hammer the nails into the wall where you want
to have the calendar and hang the twig from the nails.

Cut the jute into four circles, matching the size to the
gifts you have in mind. Tie the gifts up in the jute and
seal the parcels with twine. Cut four small circles out
of the black cardboard and make a hole in each using
the hole punch. Label the cardboard circles with the
numbers 1, 2, 3 and 4 in white permanent marker and
then tie the labels to the gift parcels.

Tie the parcels to the twig with more twine. Decorate
the calendar to your taste, e.g. with wooden stars or
paper shapes. We made a little garland out of twine
and spruce greens. Get creative!

TIP

Coffee bags are often made of jute. Ask your local coffee roaster if they have any old
bags to spare. You can also upcycle old fabrics or pieces of clothing instead of using jute.

G

RATITUDE

FOR
US

hristmas – a celebration of family. A time of deep rest among our family and friends, when we enjoy the sound of familiar voices reverberating through our homes and delight in the aromas of fir trees and spices indelibly linked to this season. These are the days when we often wish we could stop time, enjoy the moment and make it last.

The bright eyes of the children, as if a fairytale had come true; the carefree laughter; the sight of a beloved pet sleeping peacefully in front of a warm fire… These are the moments when we feel true joy and its magic, which roots deeply in our hearts and fills our lives with cherished memories. All too rarely we pause to think about how precious these moments are.

Let's not allow this magic to be shattered by trivial things. Instead, let's pay more close attention to the harmony that is created when we meet each other with a respectful, forgiving heart. After all, none of us are perfect. Advent is a time for clarity, closeness and affection – it's a time for coming together. Every year, Advent offers us the opportunity to find each other and to make this season the most beautiful of the year, laying the ground for a peaceful start to the next.

LENTIL SHEPHERD'S PIE WITH SWEET POTATO

A British classic, updated here with a hearty lentil and vegetable stew and a fluffy sweet potato topping. Served steaming hot right out of the oven, this pie is delicious as a main or as a tasty side dish.

Serves 4 (generously)

3 sweet potatoes, about 1 kg (2 lb 4 oz)
Sea salt
1 leek
1 onion
2 carrots
1 garlic clove
1 tbsp vegetable oil
1 cup (200 g) dried red lentils
½ cup (100 g) tinned corn kernels, drained
1 tbsp tomato paste (concentrated purée)
100 ml (3½ fl oz) red wine
1 tbsp Worcestershire sauce
300 ml (10½ fl oz) vegetable stock
Freshly ground black pepper
20 g (¾ oz) butter
50 ml (1½ fl oz) milk

Peel and dice the sweet potato. Cook in a saucepan of boiling salted water for 15 minutes or until soft.

Meanwhile, thoroughly wash, trim and thinly slice the leek. Peel and dice the onion and carrots. Peel and crush the garlic. Heat the vegetable oil in a large frying pan over medium heat. Briefly sauté the onion and garlic. Stir in the lentils, carrots, leek, corn and tomato paste and gently sweat. Deglaze with the wine, Worcestershire sauce and vegetable stock. Season with salt and pepper. Bring to the boil, then reduce the heat and simmer for 10 minutes.

Preheat the oven to 200°C (400°F). Drain the sweet potatoes, then add the butter and milk to the saucepan. Use a stick blender to mash the mixture well. Season with salt.

Transfer the lentil and vegetable mixture to a 26 x 20 cm (10½ x 8 inch) ovenproof dish and spread the sweet potato mixture on top. Bake for 20 minutes, then switch to the grill function and grill until the top turns golden brown.

Remove the pie from the oven, divide into portions and serve.

TIP

Shepherd's pie goes particularly well with a fresh lamb's lettuce salad drizzled with a fruity dressing.

WINTER CHILLI
(CON & SIN CARNE)

With or without meat, this chilli stew warms both body and soul. It reheats
beautifully, making it perfect for guests arriving at different times.

Serves 4

For the chilli:

2 onions
1 red capsicum (pepper)
1 garlic clove
2 tbsp canola oil
500 g (1 lb 2 oz) beef mince
Sea salt
Freshly ground black pepper
3 tbsp tomato paste
   (concentrated purée)
300 ml (10½ fl oz) vegetable
   stock
400 g (14 oz) tin diced tomatoes
1⅔ cups (330 g) tinned corn
   kernels, drained
400 g (14 oz) tin kidney beans
2–3 medjool dates, pitted
20 g (¾ oz) dark chocolate
1 pinch ground cinnamon
1 tsp ground cumin
Chilli flakes

For the topping:

1 avocado
150 g (5½ oz) crème fraîche
Juice of ½ lime
1 bunch coriander (cilantro)

*To prepare the 'sin carne' version, put 150 g (5½ oz) textured
vegetable protein (TVP) in a bowl. Add 400 ml (14 fl oz) hot water
seasoned with 1–2 tablespoons of vegetable stock. Set aside to soak
for 10 minutes. Use instead of the meat in the recipe.*

Peel and finely dice the onions. Wash, trim, seed and dice the
capsicum. Peel and crush the garlic. Heat the canola oil in a large
saucepan over high heat. Add the beef (or the soaked TVP) and
briefly fry. Season with salt and pepper. Add the diced onion
and capsicum and sauté until translucent. Stir in the garlic and
tomato paste and mix well.

Deglaze the pan with the vegetable stock and diced tomatoes
and stir thoroughly. Add the drained corn and the kidney beans
with their liquid and bring to the boil. Finely chop the dates and
add to the saucepan together with the chocolate. Gently simmer
over medium heat for 15 minutes.

Meanwhile, halve the avocado for the topping, remove the
stone and transfer the flesh to a bowl. Mash with the crème
fraîche, lime juice, salt and pepper until smooth. Wash and
coarsely chop the coriander.

Season the stew with the cinnamon, cumin and chilli flakes,
adding more salt, pepper or chilli to taste. Divide among bowls,
top with a dollop of the avocado mash and garnish with the
chopped coriander.

POMEGRANATE & GIN PUNCH

While mulled wine is always popular, why not try something different?
We suggest you branch out to a fruity-fresh punch that not only tastes
delicious, but will also warm you and your loved ones through
and through on a cold winter's night.

Serves 4

3 pomegranates
4 cups (1 litre) cloudy
  apple juice
300 ml (10½ fl oz)
  ginger beer
1 organic orange
2 star anise
3 cinnamon sticks
150 ml (5 fl oz) gin

Halve the pomegranates and juice the halves using a lemon juicer. Transfer the pomegranate juice, apple juice and ginger beer to a large saucepan.

Peel off 3–4 strips of orange zest with a vegetable peeler and add these to the saucepan. Halve and juice the orange. Add the orange juice, star anise and cinnamon sticks to the saucepan. Gently heat the mixture over low heat for about 20 minutes. Don't let the liquid boil!

Divide the punch among mugs and top each with a generous shot of gin.

TIP

This punch is particularly memorable when shared
with friends over a campfire on a cold night.

MOIST ALMOND & COCONUT CAKE

A delectably moist, soft little cake conjured up from just a few ingredients. Why not spontaneously invite a few friends over for afternoon tea or coffee and spoil them with this delicate seasonal feast of almonds and coconut?

Makes an 18 cm (7 inch) cake

Butter, for the tin
4 eggs
150 g (5½ oz) raw sugar
100 g (3½ oz) desiccated coconut
2 cups (200 g) almond meal
1 tsp grated zest from an organic lemon
1 tbsp icing (confectioners') sugar

Preheat the oven to 180°C (350°F). Butter an 18 cm (7 inch) springform cake tin.

Separate the eggs. Beat the egg whites until stiff. Whisk the yolks and icing sugar until foamy. Stir in the coconut and almond meal and add the lemon zest. Fold in the beaten egg whites.

Pour the batter into the tin. Bake for 30–40 minutes. Insert a wooden toothpick to test for doneness. If none of the cake mixture sticks to the toothpick, the cake is ready. Remove from the oven and set aside to cool a little. Dust with icing sugar and serve.

TIP

Use a paper or wooden star to create a beautiful pattern: place the star on top of the cake before dusting it with the icing sugar. Once you remove the star, the pattern will have transferred to the cake.

MUSHROOM WELLINGTON WITH CHESTNUT CREAM

A roast may be the traditional choice for a Christmas feast, but this crisp,
light, puff pastry Wellington filled with fragrant mushrooms makes for a
perfect alternative for those who prefer a vegetarian or vegan option.
This pairs perfectly with a velvety chestnut cream.

Serves 4

For the Wellington:

2 French shallots
500 g (1 lb 2 oz) button
   mushrooms
2 tbsp canola oil
1 sprig rosemary
1 tsp coconut sugar
Sea salt
Freshly ground black pepper
275 g (9¾ oz) frozen (vegan)
   puff pastry, thawed
1 small garlic clove
2 tbsp mustard
2–3 tbsp (vegan) cream
   cheese

For the chestnut cream:

1 large floury potato
400 g (14 oz) precooked
   chestnuts
150 ml (5 fl oz) almond milk
50 g (1¾ oz) butter (vegan)
1 tbsp almond butter
1 tsp coconut sugar

Preheat the oven to 200°C (400°F). For the Wellington, peel
and finely dice the French shallots. Wash, trim and slice the
mushrooms. Heat the canola oil in a frying pan. Add the diced
shallots and sweat until translucent. Add the mushrooms and
rosemary. Lightly fry, then sprinkle with the coconut sugar.
Season with salt and pepper and remove the rosemary.

Roll out the puff pastry on a baking tray. Peel and crush the
garlic. Combine with the mustard and cream cheese. Spread
the pastry with the cream cheese mixture. Top half of the pastry
with the mushrooms, leaving a border of about 1 cm (½ inch).
Carefully fold in the edge and then fold the uncovered pastry
over the mushrooms. Seal the sides. Bake for about 20 minutes.

For the chestnut cream, peel and dice the potato. Add the
chestnuts and diced potato to a saucepan and cover with salted
water. Bring to the boil, then reduce the heat and simmer for
about 20 minutes or until everything mashes easily with a fork.
Drain off the water. Add 100 ml (3½ fl oz) of the almond milk
and the butter and gently heat over low heat. Once the butter
has melted, mash the potatoes and chestnuts to make a smooth
cream. Continue to stir the mixture over low heat, adding the
remaining almond milk and the almond butter. Season with
salt and coconut sugar.

Divide the mushroom Wellington among plates and serve
with the chestnut cream.

RED VELVET CRANBERRY CAKE

This festive tiered cake is bound to leave an impression, both visually and flavour-wise. Its exquisite combination of cream and fruit hits all the right notes, plus it makes for an absolute eye-catcher during the Christmas season.

Makes an 18 cm (7 inch) cake
For the cake:
250 g (9 oz) butter, softened, plus a little extra for the tin
200 g (7 oz) raw sugar
1 pinch sea salt
6 eggs
1 tsp ground vanilla
1½ tbsp red food colouring
3⅓ cups (500 g) spelt flour
4 tsp baking powder
150 ml (5 fl oz) milk
50 ml (1½ fl oz) cranberry juice (or use milk)

For the frosting:
500 g (1 lb 2 oz) cream cheese
1 cup (120 g) icing (confectioners') sugar
200 ml (7 fl oz) single (pure) cream
⅔ cup (100 g) dried cranberries

Cranberries and rosemary, for garnish (optional)

Preheat the oven to 160°C (320°F). Butter an 18 cm (7 inch) springform cake tin.

Whisk the butter, raw sugar and salt until foamy. Add the eggs and vanilla and continue whisking until creamy, then stir in the food colouring. Combine the spelt flour and baking powder and gradually fold into the butter and egg mixture, alternating with the milk and cranberry juice.

Pour the batter into the tin. Bake on the lowest rack of the oven for 1 hour. Carefully remove the cake from the tin and leave to cool completely on a wire rack.

For the frosting, put the cream cheese in a bowl. Sift the icing sugar on top and mix well. Whip the cream until stiff, then fold it into the mixture.

Carefully halve the cooled cake horizontally to make two layers. Spread the bottom half with half of the frosting. Arrange the dried cranberries on top, then replace the top cake layer. Spread the remaining frosting all over the cake. Garnish with fresh cranberries and rosemary, if desired.

Happiness
IS A MATTER OF PERSPECTIVE.
SOMETIMES WE LOSE SIGHT OF
WHAT REALLY MATTERS,
MAKING US BLIND TO TRUE JOY,
EVEN THOUGH IT'S ALL AROUND US.

GREEN WINTER STEW WITH PIKELETS

This hearty stew is a great energy booster. We serve it with pikelets instead of bread. Both can be easily reheated to make sure everyone is perfectly well fed and satisfied.

Serves 4

For the stew:

800 g (1 lb 12 oz) waxy
  potatoes
1 large onion
2 tbsp canola oil
1 tsp sugar
4 cups (1 litre) vegetable
  stock
2–3 bay leaves
1 tsp dried summer savoury
500 g (1 lb 2 oz) green beans
2 sprigs curly parsley
3 tbsp white wine vinegar
Sea salt
Freshly ground black pepper

For the pikelets:

2 eggs
1⅔ cups (250 g) plain
  (all-purpose) flour
200 ml (7 fl oz) milk
1 pinch sea salt
Butter, for frying

For the stew, peel and dice the potatoes. Peel and finely dice the onion. Heat the canola oil in a large saucepan over medium heat. Add the diced onion and sweat until translucent. Stir in the sugar and allow it to gently caramelise. Pour in the stock and add the potatoes, bay leaves and summer savoury. Bring to the boil, then reduce the heat to medium and simmer for about 10 minutes.

Diagonally slice the green beans into small pieces. Pick off the parsley leaves from the stems. Chop and add to the stew together with the beans and vinegar. Stir well and continue to cook over high heat until done, about 15 minutes. Remove the bay leaves and season the stew with salt and pepper.

While the stew is cooking, separate the eggs for the pikelets. Whisk the flour with the milk, egg yolks and salt to make a batter. Set aside for 15 minutes. Beat the egg whites until stiff and fold into the batter. Heat a little butter in a pan. Add a small ladleful or large spoonful of batter and allow it to spread. Once the top of the batter has set, loosen the pikelet by gently shaking the pan, then flip the pikelet over. Slide a little more butter underneath and continue to fry on the second side until golden. Repeat until all of the batter is used up. Heat the oven to about 50°C (120°F). Stack the pikelets on a plate and keep them warm in the oven.

Divide the stew among soup bowls. Either slice the pikelets into strips and divide these among the bowls or serve them whole on the side.

WHOLEMEAL APPLE GALETTE

Wholesome and rustic, fruity and sweet, this free-form galette is a healthier version of a traditional apple pie. It definitely makes for an irresistible centrepiece for festive Sunday afternoon teas.

Makes 1 round galette

150 g (5½ oz) cold butter
1⅔ cups (250 g) wholemeal spelt flour
¼ cup (50 g) raw sugar, plus extra for sprinkling
1 tsp ground cinnamon, plus extra for dusting
1 pinch fine sea salt
2 apples
Icing (confectioners') sugar, for dusting

Set aside 20 g (¾ oz) of the butter. Place the flour, remaining butter, 70 ml (2¼ fl oz) cold water, the icing sugar, cinnamon and salt in the bowl of an electric mixer fitted with a dough hook. Knead until combined. Cover and refrigerate for at least 1 hour to let the dough rest.

Preheat the oven to 180°C (350°F). Halve and core the apples and cut them into thin wedges. Remove the dough from the refrigerator and roll it out about 5 mm (¼ inch) thick on a lightly floured surface. Carefully transfer the dough to a baking tray lined with baking paper. Arrange the apple slices on top, leaving a border of at least 3 cm (1¼ inches). Fold in the edge to partially cover the outer apple slices. Dot the galette with the reserved butter and sprinkle with cinnamon and raw sugar.

Transfer to the oven and bake for about 40 minutes. Remove and leave to cool a little. Serve dusted with icing sugar.

TIP

This galette tastes even more delicious with a dollop of cream or coconut cream.

C

CHRISTMAS
IS A FEELING THAT
LIVES IN THE HEART.

BAKED RED CABBAGE WITH PULLED JACKFRUIT

A traditional recipe with a modern twist. Why not try something new and roast jackfruit, a recent culinary rediscovery, instead of meat?

Serves 4

250 g (9 oz) tinned green
  jackfruit
1 tsp sweet paprika
1 tsp fresh thyme leaves
1 tsp fresh oregano leaves
2 tsp mustard
2 tbsp tomato paste
  (concentrated purée)
Sea salt
Freshly ground black pepper
1 red cabbage
90 ml (3 fl oz) olive oil
1 garlic clove
1 onion
2 tbsp canola oil
75 ml (2¼ fl oz) barbecue
  sauce
1 handful baby spinach
  leaves
4 large slices of sourdough
  bread

Preheat the oven to 220°C (425°F). Drain the jackfruit in a colander, then trim off the hard ends and pull the soft flesh into shreds. Toss the pulled jackfruit with the paprika, thyme, oregano, mustard and tomato paste in a bowl. Season with salt and pepper.

Trim the cabbage and cut it into eight wedges. Brush each cabbage wedge with olive oil and season with salt and pepper. Arrange the wedges on a baking tray lined with baking paper and bake for 40–45 minutes.

Meanwhile, peel the garlic and onion. Crush the garlic and finely dice the onion. Heat the canola oil in a frying pan. Add the diced onion and sweat until translucent. Stir in the garlic and shredded jackfruit and continue to fry briefly. Finally, stir in the barbecue sauce. Spread the mixture on another tray lined with baking paper. Once the cabbage has cooked for 30 minutes, slide the jackfruit tray into the oven above the cabbage and continue to roast both for another 10–15 minutes.

Pick through and wash the spinach. Arrange the cabbage and jackfruit on plates and garnish with the spinach. Serve with sourdough bread.

TIP

Jackfruit is also available precooked. Check the packaging for the suggested basic recipe and then season it as described in the recipe above.

CREAMY CAULIFLOWER & ALMOND SOUP

This delicate, creamy cauliflower soup has a lovely almond flavour that combines perfectly with the herbed garlic oil. It makes for a delectable winter lunch or supper, served with or without smoked salmon.

Serves 4

½ onion
500 g (1 lb 2 oz) cauliflower
2 tbsp canola oil
2 cups (500 ml) vegetable
   stock
Sea salt
Freshly ground black pepper
2 tsp fresh oregano leaves
2 tsp fresh thyme leaves
½ garlic clove
100 ml (3½ fl oz) olive oil
300 ml (10½ fl oz) almond
   milk
1 pinch freshly grated
   nutmeg
Grated zest of ½ organic
   lemon
1 tbsp almond butter
4 tbsp crème fraîche
1 dash lemon juice
4 slices smoked salmon

Preheat the oven to 180°C (350°F). Peel and dice the half onion. Trim and coarsely chop the cauliflower. Set aside two handfuls. Heat 1 tablespoon of the canola oil in a large saucepan, add the diced onion and sweat until translucent. Stir in the cauliflower and continue to sauté. Stir in the vegetable stock and bring to the boil, then reduce the heat and simmer the vegetables for about 15 minutes.

Meanwhile, divide the remaining cauliflower into small florets. Toss with 1 tablespoon of the canola oil in a bowl. Sprinkle the florets with sea salt, pepper and 1 teaspoon each of the oregano and thyme. Spread on a baking tray lined with baking paper. Transfer to the oven and roast until golden, about 15 minutes.

Meanwhile, peel and crush the half garlic clove and pound to a paste with the remaining herbs, salt and olive oil.

Once the cauliflower in the saucepan is cooked, stir in the almond milk and season everything with salt, pepper and grated nutmeg. Add the lemon zest and almond butter. Blend the soup with a stick blender until creamy. Keep warm until serving.

Season the crème fraîche with salt, pepper and lemon juice. Thinly slice the salmon. Divide the soup among bowls. Garnish with the crème fraîche and serve with the roasted cauliflower, herbed garlic oil and salmon. Serve hot.

RAIN IN ITS
LOVELIEST FORM.

TABLE GARLAND

A little bohemian Christmas magic with uniquely rustic charm.
This lovely arrangement of evergreen foliage and individual candles
makes for a naturally stylish table decoration that is perfect
for a relaxed feast.

Greenery of your choice,
(e.g. fir, eucalypts, etc.)
Ribbon
Tall candle holders
Candles

Set out your greenery lengthways along the centre of the table, interlacing the stems as best you can. Cut a few short lengths from your ribbon, about 4 cm (1½ inches) each, to tie the stems together here and there so that they won't come apart during the feast. Arrange the candle holders in between and next to the garland. Add the candles.

We like to set out our garland in a wavy line, which not only provides perfect spaces for the candles, but also looks more natural.

TIP

If you like, add bows, baubles or other Christmas decorations to your garland.

117

SALT DOUGH DECORATIONS

Salt dough Christmas decorations, which were all the rage in the 1980s, deserve to be updated for the 21st century. The dough is very quick and easy to make and hugely fun for children to work with in the pre-Christmas season. Salt dough decorations also make great gifts, but it's just as much fun to stash them away for a year, only to rediscover and reminisce over them next Christmas.

2 cups (300 g) flour –
  white type 405 flour for
  light-coloured decorations
  or wholemeal type 1050
  flour for darker ones
1 cup (220 g) fine salt
1 cup (250 ml) water
1 tbsp sunflower or
  canola oil
½ cup (90 g) potato flour
  (optional, but it makes the
  dough more pliable)
Ribbons for threading
Colour for painting
  (optional)

Preheat the oven to 130°C (250°F). Add all ingredients to a mixing bowl, combine and knead very well. Once the dough is soft and pliable, roll it out about 5 mm (¼ inch) thick. Cut out your favourite cookie shapes and transfer them to a baking tray lined with baking paper. Use a toothpick to make holes for attaching ribbons or twine later. Make sure you leave enough distance to the edges so that they won't tear.

Transfer your little works of art to the oven and bake for about 30 minutes. Once cooled, the decorations turn hard so you can paint them or decorate them with your favourite ribbons.

TIP

Add a few nice beads for a lovely decorative effect. Pull a ribbon through the prepared hole and string a bead onto it on either side. Hold the beads in place by tying the ribbon in knots, then tie the ribbon ends together.

PLACE CARDS

Pretty place cards make for a very special and personal welcome for your guests and put a smile on their face even before they sit down to your feast. They are a way of expressing the host's joy in, and appreciation of, the shared company, especially when the host took the time and effort to make them by hand.

*Small sprigs of fir or cypress
    (one per guest)*
Green floral wire
Black craft paper
Scissors
Hole punch
*White permanent marker
    or crayon*
Black twine

Shape the fir or cypress sprigs, one per guest, into small rings about 5–7.5 cm (2–3 inches). Hold these together with a little wire.

Cut the craft paper into 5 cm (2 inch) circles. Use a hole punch to make a hole in each of the circles, about 5 mm (¼ inch) from the edge. Write the guest names onto the paper circles with permanent marker or crayon and attach the circles to the twig rings with twine.

Arrange the place cards on your festively set table.

TIP

Feel free to experiment with different types of foliage, coloured paper or twine – use whatever you like best.

WE FAREWELL THIS YEAR SOFTLY.
CALMLY AND CLEARLY, WE PREPARE
FOR NEW DREAMS, NEW PLANS, NEW OPPORTUNITIES,
NEW PATHS AS EXCITING AS LIFE ITSELF.
UNTIL WE MEET AGAIN NEXT YEAR –
ON CANDLE-LIT WINTRY NIGHTS.

INDEX OF RECIPES

INDEX OF INGREDIENTS

INDEX OF INGREDIENTS

ABOUT THE AUTHORS

Advent is the first joint book project written by the WALDSINNIG DUO. These two friends share a great passion for creative work and a love of a slow, sustainable way of life.

KERSTIN, who generally goes by her nickname of 'Kerze', meaning 'candle', is a foodie through and through. She's on top of anything to do with food, whether it's ingredients, packaging design or the latest restaurants. Apart from food and design, Kerstin's other great passion is photography. And what better way to combine all three than by creating cookbooks! That's why Kerstin already has two cookbooks published with Hölker Verlag: *This Is Your Day* and *Eat more of what makes you happy*. Contact: *waldsinnig.de/kn.niehoff@gmail.com*

LAURA started by writing a column before embarking on this book project. Her love of deep and meaningful moods and conversations are always reflected in her writing and photography. Laura brings her eye for the little things in life and authentic connection to nature and art to her work as a content designer, often producing books that provide readers and viewers with little havens of serenity. She and her dog Candy can be frequently found in the hidden green oases of her home town of Munster, in cosy vegetarian restaurants or one of the farm shop cafés in the surrounding countryside. Contact: *waldsinnig.de/l.fleiter@mail.de*

OUR THANKS GO TO...

... our models and assistants Pia, Mareike, Norbert, Danny and Jenny.
... our mothers for their amazing support and untiring help in baking and crafting.
... Hölker Verlag. Special thanks to Dagmar, Jasmin and Franzi for the great teamwork.
... Stefanie Wawer for the stunning design.
... Katharina Wind for the finishing touches on our texts.
... our beloved canine models Candy and Barack.
... our families for their unwavering love and support. Special thanks to Lutz and Franz who give us the freedom to pursue projects of this nature.
... our guys. To Norbert for 'cleaning up after us' and Sascha for his driving services in Norway and his consistently honest feedback.

Products used in this book:
Coffee by Lenis Coffee Family *(lenis-coffee-family.de)*
Various foods by Davert *(davert.de)*
Knives by RaSch Knives *(rasch-messer.de)*

Always wash and pat dry vegetables, fruit, herbs and lettuces carefully before use.
Unless stated otherwise, bake goods on the middle rack of your oven.

TABLESPOON MEASURES: We have used European 15 ml (3 teaspoon)
tablespoon measures. If you are using a larger Australian 20 ml (4 teaspoon)
tablespoon, use 1 teaspoon less of the ingredient for each tablespoon specified.

Published in 2020 by Murdoch Books, an imprint of Allen & Unwin
First published in 2019 by Hölker Verlag

Murdoch Books Australia
83 Alexander Street
Crows Nest NSW 2065
Phone: +61 (0) 2 8425 0100
murdochbooks.com.au
info@murdochbooks.com.au

Murdoch Books UK
Ormond House, 26–27 Boswell Street
London WC1N 3JZ
Phone: +44 (0) 20 8785 5995
murdochbooks.co.uk
info@murdochbooks.co.uk

For corporate orders & custom publishing, contact our business
development team at salesenquiries@murdochbooks.com.au

Design: Stefanie Wawer
Typesetting: Helene Hillebrand
Recipes and food photography: Kerstin Niehoff
Texts and mood photography: Laura Fleiter
Editor: Jasmin Parapatits
Prepress: FSM Premedia, Munster

Publisher: Corinne Roberts
Translator: Claudia McQuillan-Koch, except page 24 by Christopher Newton
English-language editor: Justine Harding

© 2019 Hölker Verlag, in Coppenrath Verlag GmbH & Co. KG
Hafenweg 30, 48155 Munster, Germany
All rights reserved, also for text extracts

ISBN 978 1 76052 550 7 Australia
ISBN 978 1 91163 269 6 UK

A catalogue record for this book
is available from the National
Library of Australia

A catalogue record for this book is available from the British Library

Printed in Spain by Estella Print

10 9 8 7 6 5 4 3

MIX
Paper from
responsible sources
FSC® C009279

The paper in this book is FSC® certified.
FSC® promotes environmentally responsible,
socially beneficial and economically viable
management of the world's forests.